Blake's GO GUIDES

WRITING ESSAYS and REPORTS

Stephen McLaren

PASCAL
PRESS

ISBN 978 1 87708 520 8

Pascal Press
PO Box 250
Glebe NSW 2037
(02) 8585 4044
www.pascalpress.com.au

Publisher: Vivienne Joannou
Series editor: Emma Driver and Ian Rohr
Edited by Jo Avigdor
Page design, layout and cover by DiZign Pty Ltd
Photos by Brand X, Eyewire, Ingram Publishing and PhotoDisc
Printed by Green Giant Press

A NOTE FROM THE PUBLISHER

We live in a world where the ability to communicate well is highly valued. Essays and reports are the main ways we communicate about more complex and detailed subjects. If you can improve your skills and techniques in this area, your audience — whether it be teachers, employers or a wider audience — will be able to grasp more fully what you are trying to say. In any communication some of the meaning is lost or changed from one person to the next, but you can minimise this by clear, well-structured essays and reports.

As with all of our Go Guides, we aim to bring you the greatest amount of really useful information in the shortest number of pages. After all, who has time to read 300-page books about essays and reports? If you have a writing task to do, you want to spend as much time on the task itself — not just preparing for it. So this book is designed to give you quick access to the ideas and skills you need without the padding that so many self-help books contain.

If you have any comments on how this book could be improved, please don't hesitate to email me at matthew@pascalpress.com.au.

Matthew Blake
Publisher

ABOUT THE AUTHOR

Stephen McLaren is the author of two successful textbooks on writing: *HSC Essay Writing made Easy* (1995, 2nd edition 2001) and *Quicksmart Easy Writer: A Student's Guide to Essays and Reports* (1997), both for Pascal Press.

Originally an English teacher, Stephen has been teaching Communication and Business Communication at TAFE and university for many years.

Stephen taught Professional and Academic Writing at the University of Western Sydney from 1993 to 1999, and currently teaches Communication at Macquarie University. He also runs a small consultancy in academic editing and research and has been a regular contributor to the ABC's *BackBerner*.

TABLE OF CONTENTS

The GRADE approach to report writing

A five-step approach to planning your report, gathering data,
organising and presenting your information, explaining and interpreting
your findings and drawing conclusions.

Further tips for success

Get help with writing essays under exam conditions and common
language issues. Includes answers to frequently asked questions about
language, grammar and writing techniques.

Further reading and resources

A list of useful books and other resources on writing and language,
including style guides, dictionaries, thesauruses and websites.

Glossary

A helpful guide to technical terms used in essay and report writing.

Index

INTRODUCTION

This guide provides a quick introduction to the basics of writing essays and reports. It presents the key principles of academic writing, explains the structure of essays and reports and examines the use of language.

This guide uses the **GRADE approach** to assignment writing, which offers a simple method for planning, researching and writing essays and reports. **Students and adult learners** have never been busier, whether at senior secondary school, TAFE or university, whether studying on-campus, on-line or by distance. The GRADE approach offers useful suggestions for **effective time management** for students and adult learners with busy lives.

It is not possible to cover all the varied expectations for academic writing in the many different fields of study. It is important to take note of **any instructions** from your teacher, tutor or lecturer and check with them if you are unsure. Once you have mastered the basics, check the suggestions for **further reading** on page 61.

WHAT MAKES A GOOD ESSAY OR REPORT?

Essays and reports are based on certain key requirements and processes which incorporate an underlying **structure**. It is important for you to understand and apply this structure. In addition, it is important that you understand your marker's expectations.

A **well-written essay or report** should be:

◆ **Relevant**. Always answer the question. Base the structure of your assignment on the question and ensure that you keep 'on topic' throughout.

◆ **Well-organised**. The more complicated your material, the more you need to structure your work carefully, to make it easy to read and understand.

◆ **Signposted**. Using linking sentences, phrases and words helps the reader to understand your argument and to see the connections between different sections of your assignment.

◆ **Cohesive**. Your writing should be consistent, clear and without internal contradictions.

◆ **Specific**. Assignments are an opportunity to show your knowledge and understanding of the subject.

◆ **Concise**. Waffle, repetition, meaningless phrases and fancy words do NOT impress the reader. Have something meaningful to say and say it.

◆ **Interpretative**. Do not cram your assignment with unexplained facts and figures or frequent, lengthy quotes. 'Interpret' your data for the reader and relate it to the argument or theme that you are developing.

◆ **Analytical/critical**. Do not assume that your first impression is necessarily right. Examine the data carefully and base your conclusions on an objective consideration of the facts.

◆ **Well-expressed**. A well-written work that is a pleasure to read is worthy of a better grade. With few exceptions, academic writing can be made comprehensible with simple, clear expression. It is NOT about trying to impress with a stream of jargon. (However, learning to use the language and thinking of the discipline is certainly important.)

◆ **Complete**. Don't obsess over word limits or try to write the least amount possible. Aim to write an assignment that is self-contained and that meets the requirements.

Assignments are usually **developed in stages** from planning through a series of drafts. That is one of many reasons why **time management** is so important. You need to allow time for your understanding to grow as you read and think about the topic.

Writing a good essay or report will involve **three main processes**:

A Stating your **proposition** (the central argument of your essay)
B Supporting your proposition with **evidence**: facts and ideas
C Explaining the **significance** of what you have written.

The **essay genre** uses this structure with a **Introduction-Body-Conclusion** layout. **Reports** have a similar structure. **Business writing** genres such as letters and memos also follow this pattern. Even a paragraph can follow this three-step form by starting with a **topic sentence**, elaborating with supporting **evidence** and concluding with a **mini-summary**. This pattern can also be followed when drafting a short answer in an exam.

Why is most formal writing structured like this? It is because the reader has **three primary needs**:

◆ To understand what you are trying to **say immediately**
◆ To see the **evidence** for themselves so they can test your reasoning
◆ To **see the point** of what you are trying to say.

Whenever you are stuck, these three steps will help you get started again. Ask yourself: What am I trying to say? What evidence do I have? So what?

ESSAYS: A SHOWCASE
OF YOUR ABILITY

What is an essay?

The four types of writing are:

- description
- narration (story)
- exposition (explanation)
- argument.

Essays can be based on any one of these types or on a combination of them. However, the most common academic essay form is the **argument-based essay** which is the focus of this guide.

> The essay is a sustained **argument** weighing the evidence about an idea or a question and creating a full and satisfying conclusion.

Key terms

Let us look at some key terms:

- **Argument**. The essay states a **proposition** in answer to a question or advances a **thesis** where no specific question was asked. For convenience, the term 'proposition' is used throughout this guide. The proposition is your **main line of thought**, the backbone of the essay, what it is 'about'. A proposition which is supported by detailed, logical discussion is called an 'argument'.

> An argument is a proposition, supported by evidence and logic.

- **Sustained**. It is relatively easy to provide a simple one-sentence answer to a question. However, it is far more demanding to **develop that answer** into a sustained response that gathers momentum and becomes more convincing as it goes into greater depth. Your essay will be assessed not merely on what you know. It is also a test of your **capacity to reason**; to bring together different pieces of information in a meaningful way; to argue a case; to make judgements; to analyse data and to express yourself in formal language. The essay is a **showcase** of your ability!

- **Full conclusion**. In the best essays, conclusions bear fruit. They go beyond a summary of the discussion by looking at the **point** of those conclusions and their **significance**. If your essay leaves the reader feeling unconvinced or thinking 'What of it?' then it has basically failed. Many teachers and lecturers, when deciding on a final essay mark, will re-read the introduction and conclusion and ask themselves: 'What does this essay promise to show? Does it deliver on this promise?'

The essay question

An essay question can be described as 'open' or 'closed': the more specific the essay question is, the more closed it is.

A **closed essay question** is easier to answer because it tells you what to do and what matters to address. An **open question** makes you rely on your own knowledge and understanding to decide what matters to discuss and how. In this sense an open question is more demanding, but you have the advantage of greater choice in your response.

This question is quite 'open':

> *What impact did the advent of television have on Australian society in the 1960s and '70s?*

This question is relatively 'closed':

> *What impact did the advent of television have on social cohesion and participation in Australian society in the 1960s and '70s? Discuss, with reference to three theories of social capital.*

Key words in the essay question

To make sure you understand the question correctly, look out for the key words. There are **four main kinds** of key words and an essay question will contain some or all of them. Three kinds of key words specify the **broad or specific content** you should address, while the fourth gives instructions on **what to do**.

All four kinds of key words are contained in the following example.

> *'I've stopped aiming for perfect communication; it doesn't exist. What I do aim for is effective communication, on which I insist.' (CEO of a large Australian organisation) Is perfect communication possible in the workplace? Explain, giving examples of communication breakdown and how they can be avoided.*

Subject key words define the broad area of study. The subject in the above question is 'Organisational Communication'. While subject keywords are not always specified, it is always worthwhile remembering the broad context of the question. An answer to the above question would be missing the mark if it described communication in general but ignored the specific focus on organisational structure, types of communication within an organisation and so on.

Topic key words specify what part of the subject you should discuss. The question's topic is 'effective communication', a key goal within most organisations.

Aspect key words specify a focus on one particular part of that topic. The essay question directs you to look at one aspect, 'communication breakdown'. Though you are not restricted to that aspect only, you must cover it.

Instruction key words specify what you are asked to do, for example, 'explain', 'discuss', and 'compare'. The question asks you to 'explain' your views about 'perfect communication' and to 'give examples' of communication breakdown.

The following **sample** demonstrates some of the basic features of the essay structure. In particular, look at:

- Use of **key words** from the essay question
- Continuous **line of argument** from introduction through to conclusion
- Use of **topic sentences**, **formal language**, **linking words** and **phrases**.

Sample essay

Which is more important to the successful essay:
appropriate use of language or a well-developed argument?

The essay is a structured form of writing used in various learning institutions. While requirements vary according to the course of study, writing a successful essay involves more than just quickly answering a question. As a display of one's writing skills, knowledge and understanding, the essay relies equally on the appropriate and precise use of language and on the development of a reasoned argument. The importance of written language can be attributed in part to the nature of formal written communication and to the marker's expectations. However, a 'word-perfect' essay that is not based on a satisfactory response to the question, supported by research and logical discussion, is an empty essay. An essay without a well-developed argument will be confused and ineffective.

To understand the importance of language to the essay, it is valuable to contrast spoken communication with written communication. In particular, the roles of feedback and non-verbal communication illustrate that written communication has little means of communicating beyond language itself.

Spoken communication often works as a two-way dialogue; the hearer can respond, ask questions and clarify any confusion. In written communication, however, the reader has no opportunity for feedback, so the language must be clear and self-explanatory.

Nonverbal communicative messages are constantly being sent between speaker and listener in person-to-person conversation. These include tone of voice, facial expressions, gestures, body language and other ways of illustrating meaning. Thus, spoken conversation readily compensates for any shortcomings in the use of words. Even in a telephone conversation, tone of voice and other non-verbal cues assist communication. The essay writer, however, cannot use these extra tools and must rely on language alone.

Another consideration is that listeners tend to be very forgiving of language errors in spoken communication because meaning is also conveyed by other means. Some experts believe that 65 percent of the message in interpersonal communication is nonverbal (Knapp, 1980, quoted in Mohan, McGregor and Strano: 1992, 53). It is easy to understand why a common piece of advice in textbooks is NOT to write as we speak (Osland, Boyd, McKenna and Saluszinsky: 1991, 1) and one reason that many people find writing difficult at first is that they are not used to paying close attention to language.

In addition, spoken communication usually does not leave a permanent trace. Written pieces, however, are a record of words used and can be examined quite closely. Because the essay is usually assessed and graded, language is a marking consideration and the marker is likely to notice both strengths and weaknesses. Since the so-called 'mechanical' aspects of language are one indicator of the writer's skill, grammar, punctuation, spelling, referencing and so on may affect the final mark. Therefore it is obvious that the appropriate use of language is a major concern. However, good use of language alone does not make a successful essay. The essay must demonstrate a satisfactory level of knowledge and understanding within a reasoned argument.

Two early definitions of 'essay' were 'to try' or 'to weigh'. The essay writer must explore a question and 'try' possible responses until the most satisfactory answer is found. Likewise, the evidence for and against a proposition, or for two alternative arguments, should be 'weighed' up. Both these early meanings indicate that the essay was designed to engage with knowledge and thought, by exploring and examining evidence. Without this, the essay is empty.

Structure is an essential feature of the essay, since ideas must be explained and discussed in a logical sequence. An essay that does not develop an argument becomes a jumble of facts and ideas. Even if each fact and thought has obvious, direct relevance to the question, a 'stream of consciousness' flow does not create a satisfactory answer. The argument is what shapes the essay throughout. Indeed, even if the language is unclear in parts, understanding the argument helps the reader to interpret that passage better.

Ornate language will not save an essay that is too general, illogical or simply wrong. While it is possible to 'write around' an essay topic in the broadest, vaguest terms, most markers quickly notice a lack of substance. Again, while it is helpful to use the specific language of a particular discipline, it is only possible to do so correctly if you understand it properly. A common mistake of students is to lose their 'natural voice' in their writing. They try to copy the complicated sentences and words of the authors they are reading, only to lose control of the language (Bate and Sharpe: 1996, 61). In this respect, the ideas and evidence supporting the argument are as important as language itself.

Indeed, students usually find that the more developed their thoughts, the clearer their written expression becomes. Therefore, a well developed argument, and the knowledge and analysis that created it, aids the sometimes slow process of finding the best expression.

It has been demonstrated that the appropriate use of language, and a well-developed argument, are equally important in creating a successful essay. Written communication makes more demands on the writer and reader than does spoken communication on the speaker and listener. Clear language is crucial in the essay. This is especially so because the essay sometimes addresses abstract and involved subjects. Equally however, an essay that does not answer the question in any depth, or that is unstructured and haphazard in approach, cannot be called 'successful'. The right use of language in an essay is to serve a well-developed argument. An argument is only 'good' when it has been fully explained and communicated clearly to the reader.

References

Bate, D. and Sharpe, P. (1996). *Writer's Handbook for University Students* (2nd edn). Nelson Thomson Learning, Melbourne.

Knapp, M.L. (1980). *Essentials of non-verbal communication*. Holt, Rinehart and Wilson, New York.

Mohan, T., McGregor, H. and Strano, Z. (1992). *Communicating! Theory and Practice* (3rd edn). Harcourt Brace Jovanovich, Sydney.

Osland, D., Boyd, D., McKenna, W. and Saluszinsky, I., (1991). *Writing in Australia: A Composition Course for Tertiary Students*. Harcourt Brace Jovanovich, Sydney.

Essay structure

The standard essay has three parts: **Introduction, Body and Conclusion**.

Introduction

Many essay writers find it hard to get started. Getting the introduction right is all-important because it is here that you **lay the foundations** for your essay. A clear introduction provides a mini 'plan' to refer to if you get stuck. Your introduction should:

- Demonstrate that you have **understood** the question
- State your **proposition**
- Outline **key points** of your argument
- Prepare **the way ahead** for your essay.

Useful **techniques** for writing your **introduction** include the following:

- **Use the key words**. From the start, reassure your marker that you have understood the question and are going to answer it. Without simply parroting the question, make sure your introduction includes key words that respond to the question as a whole.
- **State your proposition**. Indicate your response concisely, without going into detail. In the sample essay above, the broad question is whether language or argument is most important to the successful essay. The proposition advanced is that they are equally important.
- **Indicate the key points supporting your proposition**. Briefly indicate the main 'proofs' you will advance so that the reader can quickly relate the discussion in the body of the essay to your argument. The sample essay's introduction indicates that first language then argument will be discussed, in relation to:

  - The nature of formal written communication
  - The expectations of the marker
  - The importance of knowledge and logical discussion
  - The role of the argument in an effective written piece.

  The essay then treats each of those points in turn.

- **Anticipate your conclusion**. Apart from signposting the argument, you can also foreshadow your conclusion in the introduction. While not essential, this helps the reader to fully grasp your argument from the start and see where the essay is heading.

Body

In the body of the essay you **develop a detailed argument** supporting your proposition as well as clarifying and qualifying it. Unlike a report, an essay does not include headings, so it is important to write clearly to signal where the discussion is going and to carefully structure the explanation of supporting evidence.

There are different ways of **organising information** in an essay. One of the most common organisational principles is to rank your points **in order of importance**, either starting from the least powerful point and building momentum up to the most compelling, or starting with the strongest point first for impact then reinforcing it with other points.

Apart from order of importance, there are a variety of other **organisational principles** you might use in your essay:

- **From broad to specific**. It is usual to provide an overview or background information before going into detail.
- **Chronological (time) order**. A history essay might discuss events and movements in chronological sequence.
- **Geographical/spatial**. A description of the terrain of a country could proceed from west to east, then from north to south. You could describe the design of a house starting from the exterior then moving to the interior, from room to room, from front to back.
- **Cause-effect**. The argument of an essay might trace a causal chain: a series of events and the effects they create.
- **Comparison**. A discussion comparing two different things might be based on particular criteria. For example, if you were asked to compare Macintosh computers and PCs, you would set out a number of objective measurements and compare how each rates against them.

It is important to **organise your information** within each section of the body of your essay. Arranging your notes into **groups** according to themes will help organise your mind too. The sample essay on the previous pages would be supported by a series of notes under the following headings: comparison of interpersonal communication to written communication; a marker's expectations; the nature of the essay; structure of the essay; importance of 'content'.

The essay question on page 10 asks you to agree or disagree with the proposition that perfect communication is impossible, and to explain your view with reference to communication breakdown in the workplace. An outline of notes for this essay follows.

Sample essay notes

Effective communication
- Definition (from textbook)
- Importance of effective communication

- Consequences of ineffective communication

Perfect communication
- Importance of setting goals
- How organisations aim for perfection but rarely get there
- How/why unrealistic expectations can be a problem
- 'To give up the ideal of good communication is not to admit defeat' (quote)

Communication breakdown
- Diagram of transactional model of communication
- Explain how a weakness in any single link of the communication chain can cause 'noise' and distort the signal
- Give examples of communication breakdown
- Analyse why they happened, in terms of the model of communication
- Explain how communication breakdown could have been avoided

Conclusions
- Explain how imperfect communication can nonetheless become effective
- Why must we insist on effective communication?

When writing **the body** of the essay, it is important not to lose track of the question or your own argument. The following suggestions will help you avoid this.

- ◆ **Use topic sentences**. Topic sentences are important not only in an essay or report but also in most formal writing. They form the **backbone of each paragraph**, just as the argument forms the backbone of the essay as a whole. Topic sentences often begin the paragraph, **introducing the theme**. (They can, however, appear anywhere in the paragraph). They give shape to your writing, help create order within paragraphs (and often between them) and allow the reader and skim-reader to **absorb the main idea** rapidly. Avoid messy paragraphs which unload information without having any clear point to them.

- ◆ **Highlight the topic sentences**. Do this in each paragraph when you revise your draft essay. If you can't find one, write one. This might involve **reshaping** the entire paragraph. If you 'lose the plot', try writing a topic sentence to define your point.

- ◆ **Make mini-summaries at the end of each point**. Once you have finished a section, **sum up briefly** before turning to the next. For example: 'Thus, it is evident that ... '
         'It has been established that ... '

The **sample essay** briefly sums up the importance of language before linking the second main item of discussion, that is, the importance of argument: 'Therefore it is evident that the appropriate use of language is a paramount concern. However, good use of language alone does not make a successful essay ... '

- ◆ **Use 'transition' or linking words and phrases**. These show the **logical connection** between points and help to keep you on track in developing the argument. Examples of transitions or linking words and phrases include:
    Causal: 'Consequently ... '
    Chronological: 'Subsequently ... '
    Logical: 'Therefore ... ' or 'As a result of this ... '
    Priority: 'An even more important reason was ... '

The **sample essay** uses 'however' in the first paragraph to signify a link between the first part of the proposition (language is very important) and the second part (argument is equally important).

- ◆ **Refer back to your argument**. Demonstrate how the point under discussion **relates to your argument**. Do this when you introduce each point and when you conclude discussion of that point.
- ◆ **Give specific proof**. Making mere assertions (claims of fact) is not enough unless you support them with evidence and reasoning. Unless what you are saying is definitely well known or quite obvious, it's better to back it up with a **reference**, a **quote** or other **explanation**.
- ◆ **Paragraph carefully**. Pages without paragraphs create a woefully disorganised effect. Thoughtful paragraphing is important because it makes an essay much easier to read. Because essays do not use headings, they are less 'reader friendly', so it is very important to break up the mass of words. **Start a new paragraph** whenever you start a new point. Whenever you write a topic sentence, this is a likely place for a new paragraph. While topic sentences keep us to the point, paragraphing reminds us to separate point from point, to show where one topic ends and the next begins.
- ◆ **Check paragraph length and format**. There is **no ideal or 'correct' length** for paragraphs, although in recent years the preference has been for shorter – six to seven lines – rather than longer ones. Half a page is very long while three lines is usually too short! **'Full block justification'** format is common in learning institutions. In this format, every line begins at the left margin with a new paragraph being

signalled by a line space. Some schools prefer the **traditional style**: indenting paragraphs at least a centimetre, with no spaces between paragraphs. Check any style requirements and be consistent whichever system you use. If your teacher or lecturer stipulates a formatting style you should follow it.

◆ **Qualify your statements**. Carefully weigh up what you are saying and restrict your claims to what is **reasonable.** Avoid statements beginning with: 'It is obvious that' or 'All ... ' unless you are quite certain of what you are saying.

Conclusion

An effective conclusion can determine the difference between a better grade and an average grade. In the best essays, conclusions do not simply restate the argument. They afford an opportunity to complete your case, to make a final statement that **leaves a lasting impression** – the sense that you have delivered a worthy outcome to your argument. It is all too common however, for an essay to peter out, letting the reader down just as it seemed to promise more.

While you should not introduce new material in the conclusion, it is allowable to develop your ideas further, based on the preceding discussion. Make sure that your conclusion appears to be **a logical development** of the argument and is relevant to the question.

THE GRADE APPROACH TO
ESSAY WRITING

The **five steps** to writing an essay are summed up in the GRADE approach:

1 **G**et to work with a plan
2 **R**esearch with a purpose
3 **A**rrange your information and develop an argument
4 **D**raft the essay in the appropriate form and structure
5 **E**dit: revise and rewrite.

Note the emphasis on **time management** incorporated in these five steps. There are many reasons why this skill is so important: handing in your work punctually and ensuring adequate time for research and for your ideas to develop fully are just some of them! The **calendar** on the following page provides a **suggested timeline** for an essay due in three weeks.

   Key principles of time management are:

◆ Start your planning and research **straight away**
◆ Allow **plenty of time** for your ideas to mature and to complete additional drafts or extra reading as required
◆ Do a **little work each day**, even if your busy schedule tempts you to leave everything until the one day of the week that is free
◆ Always **submit** your work **on time**.

1 Get to work with a plan
Analyse the question

Start on the assignment as soon as you receive it. Never sit and wait for inspiration to come – inspiration will emerge from the work that you do. Your first task is to analyse the question and work out what is required. The following **worked example** is based on this essay question:

> *'I've stopped aiming for perfect communication; it doesn't exist. What I do aim for is effective communication, on which I insist.' (CEO of a large Australian organisation) Is perfect communication possible in the workplace? Explain, giving examples of communication breakdown and how they can be avoided.*

TIMELINE FOR ESSAY ASSIGNMENT DUE IN **3** WEEKS

Wk	Mon	Tues	Weds	Thurs	Fri	Sat	Sun
1	**Day 1** Assignment given out Explore question, plan research	**Day 2** Find research materials: borrow books, photocopy articles etc.	**Day 3** Read research materials, take notes	**Day 4** Read research materials, take notes	**Day 5** Arrange and order information Develop argument Plan essay	**Day 6**	**Day 7**
2	**Day 8** Draft essay	**Day 9** Draft essay	**Day 10** Further reading/ re-reading	**Day 11** Revise essay	**Day 12** Work on weak points Redraft entire essay	**Day 13**	**Day 14**
3	**Day 15** Revise, redraft	**Day 16** Refine language, final fact checking and referencing	**Day 17** Final research and re-reading	**Day 18** Final draft and check presentation	**Day 19** Proofread hard copy Print good copy, attach cover sheet, title page	**Day 20**	**Day 21**
4	**Day 22** Submit essay on time						

What is this question **really asking**? What does your teacher or lecturer expect? What are the ways you can go about answering it? What is the scope of the assignment? What aspects do you need to cover and in how much detail?

This question sets out three requirements. Firstly, it asks you to state **whether or not you believe** that perfect communication is possible. Secondly, it asks you to **explain your view**. Finally, it asks you to **give examples** of communication breakdown and how it can be avoided. A satisfactory answer must respond to each part of the question.

Some people find it helpful to write themselves '**mental instructions**' to help make clear their own purpose. In the case of the above question, this would be something like: 'Explain why perfect communication is seldom achievable but effective communication is essential.' Once you have a broad understanding of what is required, **examining the key words** for this, or any other essay, will help sharpen your focus. This exercise may also prompt you **to refine or rewrite** your mental instructions. For example, you might add the following detail: 'Show how communication breakdowns can be minimised.'

Plan your research

For effective research, it is essential to have a clear idea of what you are looking for. It is therefore important to devise a **research plan**. Ask yourself what you know and what more you need to know. This will help you to absorb information more efficiently than aimlessly reading and browsing in the hope that something will jump out at you. Make your research focus **specific**. Thousands of books and papers have been written about 'communication' but only a few will relate directly to the essay question. So, researching the essay means narrowing the focus.

Next you need to search **available materials** against the key terms you are searching for. In library catalogues you would search the subheadings. For example, the word 'communication' might have subheadings relating to telecommunications, digital technology, interpersonal communication, international relations and so on. Under a subheading such as interpersonal communication, there may be sub subheadings such as workplace communication, social interaction, nonverbal communication and so on.

Your research plan could be as simple as a list of questions and key words, or detailed enough to list sources. Here is a short list for the 'Effective Communication' essay:

◆ **Basic concepts of the course** including lecture notes/class notes, course book and selected readings
◆ **Suggested readings** for the essay (where supplied)
◆ **Textbooks** on professional and organisational communication
◆ **Academic papers** on professional and organisational communication in relevant journals
◆ **Internet** materials on the subject of organisational communication with a workplace application as well as some corporate documents. Search on-line catalogues for relevant works held at other libraries and on-line resource collections in the 'communication' subject area.

2 Research with a purpose

The higher your level of study, the more important it is to research and explore the topic. Even if you don't incorporate every resource in the essay itself, it is always helpful to know a lot about your topic and to demonstrate that you have read widely and consulted a range of sources.

Assess sources quickly

We live in the so-called **Information Age**. There is so much information available on so many subjects that it is important to develop the ability to

assess each source quickly. Scan the range of resources to identify those which are likely to be useful. Ask yourself: Is it relevant to my topic? Is it up to date? Is it credible? Read the opening paragraphs to gain a quick impression of the content and the approach. Look at the publisher's blurb on the back or the author's introduction to see if a book is likely to be **relevant to your needs**. Read the abstract or summary when considering academic papers. Consult the contents pages and/or index.

There are also **ways of reading** which give you the overall 'gist' quickly, help you to follow the main theme and locate certain key terms. Examples include '**speed reading**', '**skimming**' (where the eye jumps from paragraph to paragraph focusing on topic sentences) and **scanning for particular words**. You can usually 'skim' electronic texts for certain terms by using the 'search' function on the computer. For example, if you were searching for an article about effective communication on a CD ROM, by entering the term 'effective communication' in a search box you could skip to each section where it was used.

Researching involves:
- Selecting appropriate resources
- Finding relevant sections of those resources
- Reading with a purpose
- Taking notes for a purpose

Research tips

Take a **library tour** at your learning institution to find out what is available. Many libraries offer subject-specific guides as well. When you **search** a library catalogue, CD ROM, database or Internet search engine, remember that the **search terms** you have entered may be different to the headings under which you will eventually find the information. If your search fails, try a different term. At the other extreme, if your catalogue or Internet search returns hundreds of responses, try **narrowing the search** to something closer to what you are looking for. Many electronic catalogues and search engines offer a 'help' function that gives advice on refining your search. If you still can't find the information you are after, ask the librarian for help.

Unintended plagiarism can result from poor time organisation (or perhaps laziness). Faced with a deadline and unable to locate the source, some people may be tempted to 'borrow' the words without quotation or referencing. However, it is quite easy for markers to detect this practice. **Always record all your sources** as you write your notes and reference them when quoting them in your essay. When downloading information from the Internet, always note the URL (address) of the site, the site's name and author (if known) and the date. If you are photocopying source materials, write the source information on the first photocopied page.

Reference each source according to the rules of the referencing system you are using. For more information on referencing, see page 38. When you quote a particular source, quote it word for word. If you leave words out, indicate this with an **ellipsis** (series of three dots).

Here are some **more useful research tips**:

◆ If you are having trouble finding useful sources, **ask your teacher** for suggestions.
◆ Where the essay question includes a quote, consult the **original source** of that quote.
◆ Each relevant source you consult is likely to have a **bibliography** and/ or a section including suggested further reading.
◆ Once you have found the Dewey number (a system used in a library to organise subject areas into categories) or Library of Congress reference of a relevant book, a **shelf-check** of nearby books can uncover other valuable resources.

Some useful **sources of information** are:

◆ Books and textbooks
◆ Academic journals
◆ Photocopied collections of articles held in closed reserve at the library
◆ Other works held in closed reserve at the library
◆ Reference books including atlases, encyclopaedias and dictionaries. (At the tertiary level of study, you must not rely on encyclopaedias, but such reference works can give you valuable background information.)
◆ CD ROM databases
◆ On-line discussion groups devoted to particular topics
◆ Periodicals and magazines
◆ Archives and older records such as microfiche
◆ Multimedia resources on CD ROM including encyclopaedias, educational programs, dictionaries
◆ Videos and sound recordings
◆ On-line databases and 'electronic libraries'
◆ Media websites containing archives of press stories including photographs, sound and video. (Some of these charge for usage.) The ABC has an excellent, free website with archived stories at www.abc.net.au.

The Internet

It is virtually essential for students to have access to email and the Internet these days. There are **many useful resources** on the web, including general and specialised dictionaries (for example *Bartlett's Quotations*), encyclopaedias, electronic versions of books out of copyright restrictions, and so on. You can **subscribe** to electronic publications, newsgroups or specialised on-line discussion groups. You can also **search** dissertation abstracts, check out conference proceedings and use search engines to look for particular keywords or names.

However, **treat websites with caution** as there are few guarantees of the reliability of the information they contain. Certainly do not rely solely on the Internet. Many materials can only be found in libraries, archives or museums.

Library networks

Libraries participate in major networks, so you can probably check multiple collections from your own library's **on-line catalogue**. Some institutions provide **reciprocal borrowing rights** with other educational libraries, enabling you to have your own borrower's card. If need be, enquire about inter-library loans, but be aware that they can take considerable time to arrive. Don't forget that a trip to your local library can often result in unexpected treasures, and many offer **free Internet access**.

3 Arrange your information and develop an argument

Once you have analysed the essay question and conducted your research, the next task is to outline your response. Firstly you need to digest your research and **organise the relevant data**. Secondly you need to **develop your argument**. Thirdly you should draw up an **essay plan**.

Organise your information

Ideally, you have recorded your notes under headings set out in your research plan. However if they are organised according to the source, you may need to **reorganise your notes under headings** relevant to your essay. If they are on computer it is easy to copy and paste them under different headings. **Keep track** of where you got the notes from and keep your original note files on computer disk for reference. The more information you have and the more complicated it is, the more you need to organise it. For example, you might end up with a number of **sub-groups** under some of your headings. Once your notes have been organised into headings and subheadings, **rank or order them** by importance or some other factor. Arrange the main sections in the order of discussion.

You now need to decide on a proposition in order to **develop your argument**. Remember, you can modify it later, if necessary. A **good proposition**:

◆ Answers the question comprehensively
◆ Is supported by the bulk of evidence
◆ Engages with current theories and approaches
◆ Provides an opportunity to explore the topic thoroughly.

Once you have organised your information and developed your argument, create an **essay plan**. A simple plan can comprise one sentence stating your proposition, with supporting points listed underneath in note form, finished off with a concluding sentence. A sample plan for the 'Effective Communication' essay is set out below. Note that it somewhat resembles the outline plan of notes for this essay on pages 15–16.

Sample essay plan

The importance of effective communication

Proposition: If perfect communication is seldom achievable, effective communication is essential.

Supporting points:

1 Perfect communication
  – Unless you aim high you are unlikely to reach your full potential
  – However, problems are caused by unreasonable expectations
  – Provide examples of these problems
  – Mini-conclusion: to admit imperfections is not to admit defeat

2 Consequences of poor communication
  – Damaging client relations

- Increasing risk of unnecessary problems
- Loss of business
- Bad morale within organisation

3 Effective communication
- Two contrasting definitions
- Emphasis on outcomes
- Importance of how efficiently outcomes are achieved

4 Communication breakdown
- Distortion of signal can occur anywhere in the communication chain
- Refer to transactional model of communication
- Demonstrate how different elements can all cause distortion
- Give examples of communication breakdown
- Analyse why breakdown/s occurred
- Explanation of how breakdown/s could have been avoided

Conclusion
There are so many ways that meaning can be distorted and the effect work out differently than intended that the professional communicator needs to be constantly on guard. The consequences of poor communication can have a serious effect on any organisation.

References

4 Draft the essay in the appropriate form and structure

It is only when you start to draft your essay that the **validity of your argument and the quality of your understanding** are tested fully. At the same time, the process of finding the right words to express your argument begins. The **first draft** will be roughly worded and incomplete. As you write, **mark passages** where you experience difficulty, with an asterisk or other marker, so that you can find them quickly when you revise the essay. Remember that it takes time to get the wording right.

If you are using a computer, save your first and successive drafts with file names such as PsychEssayDft1, PsychEssayDft2 etc. That way you will be able to edit the essay without losing your original material.

Draft the introduction

Key features of the **Introduction, Body and Conclusion** were discussed on pages 14-18. Here is a reminder of the important steps.

- **Introduction**. Ensure your introduction helps your reader 'tune in' and demonstrates clarity and an organised approach.

- **Key words**. Reflect back the key words from the question without parroting.
- **State your proposition**. You don't need to write: 'My proposition is ... ' or 'My thesis is ... '. It is quite acceptable to write instead: 'It will be demonstrated that ... ' or 'Examination of the evidence leads to the conclusion that ... '. Otherwise you can simply state your proposition, as in the sample essay on page 11: '... the essay relies equally on the appropriate and precise use of language and on the development of a reasoned argument.'
- **Indicate the key points supporting your proposition**. A simple mention is adequate.
- **Anticipate your conclusion (optional)**. At the time of writing your first draft, you may have no particular conclusion in mind, or just a vague idea. By the time of writing the second draft you may be able to insert a tentative conclusion.

> **TIP:** It is a common error to launch straight into your answer without establishing the foundations for the essay. Always set out your proposition and supporting points first.

Following are some **more useful tips**.

- **Define key terms which may be unclear**. This is for your benefit and for the marker who needs to see that you understand them fully. At the university or technical college level, most subjects have specialised terminology which is not adequately defined in general dictionaries. For example, the term 'communication' has many different meanings.
- **Do not go into detail in the introduction**. It is easy to get derailed by focusing on details but leave them for the body of the essay.
- **Do not get bogged down**. If you find yourself stuck at the introduction, draft the rest of the essay before coming back to it.

Draft the body

The body of the essay provides an opportunity for you to develop your argument in **greater breadth and depth**, to clarify and qualify your points, and discuss complex details. It is **not** an unstructured slab of information between the bookends of introduction and conclusion. If you have organised your data well, this will automatically lend structure to the body of your essay. Remember that your argument should follow through the entire essay in an **unbroken thread**.

A reminder of **some important points**:

- **Refer back to your argument frequently**. Your knowledge is just 'data' until you have shown its significance.

- **Use topic sentences**. This will help to keep you on track.
- **Paragraph carefully**.
- **Make mini-summaries**. Insert them at the end of each section.
- **Use 'transition' or linking words and phrases**. Essays don't have headings so you need to work harder to structure your argument.
- **Give specific proof**. Assertions (statements of views) are very weak if not supported. Generalisations such as 'Communication is extremely important' will not impress unless supported by specific evidence.
- **Qualify your statements**.

Draft the conclusion

Although you will still be coming to grips with the topic at the first-draft stage, it is still a good idea to draft a provisional conclusion at this point to help develop your thinking. Remember that the conclusion should follow logically from the preceding discussion.

The following are some **guidelines** for drafting your conclusion:

- **Re-read the question**. This will ensure you are still on track and will refresh your memory.
- **Refer back to your introduction**. Remind the reader what you have set out to 'discuss', 'argue', 'describe' and so on.
- **Summarise your argument and main points**. This could be a simple restatement if your main conclusions have been discussed in the body of the essay.
- **Complete your argument**. Take the argument further, relate it to contemporary theories, refer to particular scholars or point to implications – anything which will leave a final stamp of depth and thoroughness to do justice to your research and to your personal insights into the question. For example, you can:
  - Discuss the consequences of your argument
  - Relate the conclusion to a wider context
  - Note aspects which still remain unclear or unresolved

While there is no set rule about the **length of the conclusion**, it should be similar to the introduction or slightly longer. The body of the essay should make up the bulk of the word count. The length depends on the word limit of the essay, but a substantial conclusion is a sign that you have 'made something' of the task.

Once you have drafted the essay, **read it over again** and correct or note any obvious problems. Now give yourself a break; you've earned it!

5 Edit: revise and rewrite

Research further, and/or re-read sources

It is important to **re-read the draft** with fresh eyes. Once your first draft is completed, allow yourself a rest of at least a day or two to refresh your mind. In the meantime, while waiting for your mental batteries to recharge, an excellent practice is to **read a little more** in the subject area. The hard labour you have already put in will pay real dividends as your understanding of the topic deepens and any confusion gradually clears. Each source you consult has something different to offer, as what one source omits or explains poorly another will explain well. It is also a good idea to **re-read sources** you have already consulted as you often absorb more on a second reading.

Re-read the draft essay

Take note of your **immediate reactions** when you re-read your essay. Some passages will strike you as strong, relevant and useful. Other passages may contain an important idea that needs to be expressed more clearly or explored more thoroughly. Other passages you may now disagree with completely.

Your aim is to identify the **strengths and weaknesses** of the draft. Neither dismiss your work in despair nor applaud every word uncritically. Instead, adopt a **constructive**, **objective and positive** attitude while gradually transforming your draft into a polished, final presentation. Strengthen the stronger parts and fix the weak parts. As suggested earlier, try underlining the **topic sentence** in each paragraph. If you cannot find one, write one.

Be prepared to **let your ideas develop or change**. This will occur the more you read and the more you think about the subject. Assignments not only test your writing and understanding but are central to promoting your learning. Remember that modifying or changing your proposition and argument **does not mean failure**. Indeed, so long as the change is better, it indicates **progress and learning**.

The 'arithmetic' of revision

Part of the revision process involves **removing material** from an essay. It is often tempting to use a favourite quote or pile up a whole series of quotes, to investigate a fascinating issue or discuss your pet obsession in detail. However, **adopt a disciplined attitude** and delete everything that does not advance your argument. This is particularly important when you must observe strict word limits. Repetition of the same point or outlining vaguely related information that does not 'prove' anything relevant will not impress.

Adding material is equally important. While it is often easier to see what is unnecessary rather than what is needed, you can develop this skill. Here are some **possible additions** to make:

- A **topic sentence**
- A **quote**, supporting **reference** or other **evidence** to support an opinion
- Greater **detail** to 'nail' your point down decisively or make it clearer
- **Links between paragraphs** to show the transition from one theme to the next or to signal the point that is being made
- **Developing the theme** of a particular paragraph, or any topic, discussion point or conclusion to its logical end
- Reference to **academic concepts** and/or **theoretical perspectives** that are relevant
- **Footnotes or endnotes** (if you are using a footnoting referencing system) to explain a point or establish a reference that is relevant but not part of the actual essay
- 'Unpacking' a complicated idea by elaborating on it. Clarify what is obscure and make explicit what is not stated or only inferred.

Redraft the essay

Language use, word choice and the technical aspects of language and presentation are clearly very important in essay writing. However, there is relatively little point in worrying about the details – grammar, spelling and so on – before you have **established the structure** of the essay and **refined and fully elaborated** the argument. It's a little like cleaning and painting your new house before the builders have finished constructing it – you'll only have to do all that work again.

Your redrafting of the essay should focus on the so-called **big picture matters**: argument, structure, adequacy of research, cohesion, clarity and so on. A handy checklist is presented on page 32.

> ▶ **TIP:** Remember that, when you revise one aspect of your essay, you may need to go back and alter other parts as well.

Work on those sections you have **earmarked for attention**, first. You may need to refer back to your notes and texts or consult a new source.

Once the problem areas have been fixed, repeat the process of re-reading and redrafting the essay, paying increasing attention to **language and presentation**, until you feel you have the essay 'about right'. It is very satisfying to read over an earlier draft of an essay and see how your expression and understanding have developed.

Refine the language

Each time you rewrite part of your essay, you are refining the language as well as the argument. This process involves attention to **grammar, spelling and punctuation**, as well as vocabulary. An error-free polished style will impress while sloppiness can cost you marks.

Since we tend to **repeat our mistakes** in language usage, take careful note of **feedback** on all your essays. This is valuable information which you should use to **strengthen your understanding**, not only of the subject but also of good academic language.

The test of clear writing is whether **a reader can understand** the point you are trying to make. Some people write in a mental shorthand. 'Unpack' your words and extend them into a more complete expression of your thoughts. If need be, make the point clearer with an analogy, example or illustration. Common **language issues** are addressed on pages 55–60.

Seek feedback

If possible, ask your teacher or lecturer to **review your draft**, or at least your outline. Alternatively, ask a classmate, colleague, friend or family member. Even if they are not familiar with your subject area, the kinds of questions they ask will help you identify which passages are not as clear as they could be. Resist the temptation of briefing them on what the essay is about. If you are on track, the essay itself should do this.

The **feedback you need** is from someone who is supportive and objective, yet critical enough to bring flaws to your attention. **A word of warning**: I have seen an excellent draft changed for the worse into an unrecognisable final version. This happened because one student conferred with another and became convinced that their own ideas were completely wrong. Remember that there are usually **many satisfactory answers** to any given essay question. You are usually much better off sticking with your own approach than assuming that someone else knows better.

Professional presentation

Once your final draft is complete, don't forget the all-important details of **presentation**, including references both within the text and at the end. For more on referencing, see pages 38–39.

(See **Essay presentation checklist** on page 33.)

First draft checklist

Introduction
- ✓ Is the **question** answered?
- ✓ Is the **thesis** stated in the introduction?
- ✓ Are **supporting points** listed?
- ✓ Is a **clear argument** signalled?

Body
- ✓ Are points arranged in an easy to follow **sequence** with a logical structure?
- ✓ Are **transitions** between points clearly signalled?
- ✓ Does the discussion of each new point begin with an **introductory sentence**?
- ✓ Is each point concluded with a **mini-summary** or related to argument?
- ✓ Is **detailed evidence** used, with appropriate quotes and referencing?
- ✓ Is the essay **paragraphed**?
- ✓ Is there a **topic sentence** in each paragraph?
- ✓ Are **linking sentences** and phrases used between sections and paragraphs?
- ✓ Does the essay refer back to the argument and **stay on track** in answering the question?
- ✓ Is the argument developed in **greater depth and breadth**, not just restated?
- ✓ Is the information and discussion **relevant** in all sections?
- ✓ Is **further information** required to make the argument complete?
- ✓ Have you underlined sentences or passages which could be more **clearly expressed**?
- ✓ Have you checked **dictionary definitions** of words you are not sure about and consulted academic texts to check academic terminology?

Conclusion
- ✓ Does it refer back to the **essay question**?
- ✓ Does it echo the **proposition** announced in the introduction?
- ✓ Does it **summarise** your argument briefly?
- ✓ Does it deliver a **final statement** for extra impact?

Essay presentation checklist

- ✓ Is it **on time**? If not, contact your teacher before the due date and provide a medical certificate, note or application for extension as appropriate.
- ✓ Is the **cover sheet** filled out and attached?
- ✓ Does the essay conform to the specified **word count**? If it is significantly under, take advantage of the extra space to extend your argument. Don't pad! If it is significantly over, prune the unnecessary material.
- ✓ Have you attached a **title page**?
- ✓ Is there a **header or footer** on each page, including the page number?
- ✓ Is the **essay question** typed at the head of the essay?
- ✓ Have you used **text enhancements** consistently and appropriately (eg. bold for headings, italics for foreign words and occasional emphasis)?
- ✓ Is your **paragraph style** consistent, that is, indented or flush left?
- ✓ Are your lines **double-spaced** or as otherwise specified, eg. 1.5 line spaced?
- ✓ Have you carried out a **final check of your hard copy**, correcting any errors which have escaped you, including spacing and layout?
- ✓ Are all **quotes** in the text referenced according to a system?
- ✓ Have you included a **reference list or bibliography**?

REPORTS: INFORMATION FOR A PURPOSE

The purpose and format of reports

A report is a **structured presentation of information**, arranged and interpreted for a particular purpose. In real life, a report may give information, analyse or make recommendations (or a combination of all three).

- ◆ An **informational report** simply records the facts of the matter.
- ◆ An **analytical report** probes deeper into causes and effects. For example, an analytical report might examine economic indicators to assess the state of the economy.
- ◆ A **business report** usually provides recommendations for a course of action based on an assessment of the facts.

Unlike the essay, reports are usually **fact-based**, not argument-based. However, reports often follow a theme or a line of argument. A report which simply provides an array of data is inadequate unless it **addresses a purpose, provides relevant information and interprets that information**.

Reports come in a **wide variety of forms**. They are **focused on a purpose** which usually derives from what are called the research aims: the specific question you were asked to answer or what you have decided to find out.

While report formats differ widely, the underlying principles remain the same. Like the essay, reports have an **introduction, body and conclusion**. However, they are divided into different sections under headings.

The format can be **adapted to the subject and purpose**. A very short report will not need a contents page. Discussion of the findings can be integrated into the results section rather than having a separate section – particularly in short reports. A fact-finding or a scientific report will not necessarily have a recommendations section. Business reports are often accompanied by a covering letter but these are not usually required for academic assignments.

Follow any **specifications** set down by your teacher or lecturer such as: 'The report must include relevant graphs and tables' or 'The methodology must be explained in detail' or 'The literature review must include a search of recent electronic publications'.

If you are still unsure of how to structure your report, create a quick outline plan and ask your teacher or lecturer for feedback. They may also be able to show you a sample report.

A standard report

A standard report has the following **features**:

- Title page
- Table of contents
- List of figures or tables (where many are used)
- Abstract/executive summary
- Introduction
- Findings/results
- Discussion
- Conclusion
- Recommendations
- References and/or bibliography
- Appendices

Title page

The title page should include:

- Course/subject name and code
- Name of teacher/lecturer/tutor
- Title of assignment: for example, 'Assignment Three: Major Report into Professional Placement'
- Your name, student number and contact details
- Date.

Table of contents

A table of contents is used in larger reports. Don't forget to include page numbers. While page numbers in the body of a report are in **Arabic numerals** (1, 2, 3) the preliminary pages (located between the title page and the abstract/summary) are in lower case **Roman numerals** (i, ii, iii).

Abstract/executive summary

At the head of the report, **the abstract or executive summary** provides an overview of the entire report. It generally comprises a paragraph or two stating the report's purpose, the broad findings and conclusion. Published academic papers generally include an abstract. Business reports have an executive summary. In other reports this is simply called a summary or **synopsis**.

The abstract or summary is particularly useful because decision-makers and researchers need to grasp the gist of an academic paper or report very quickly. Likewise, your teacher or lecturer expects to see a **concise and clear account** of what your research has achieved. They are also liable to check that your summary and report match up.

Introduction

Introductions allow the reader to quickly 'tune in to' what is the often- unfamiliar subject matter of the report. In academic writing, the introduction demonstrates your grasp of the subject. The introduction formally commences the report by supplying the **necessary background information** whereas the executive summary **outlines the entire report**. It is a common mistake to write an abstract like an introduction or vice versa or simply repeat the abstract in the introduction.

As a guide, the introduction should consider the **following five points**.

◆ **Broad overview/background setting.** Give the 'big picture' or general background. Establish the grounds of the inquiry before focusing on the specific task in hand. The sample report (see pages 41–44) quickly sketches the geography and history of the town of Cheston before explaining the major challenge it now faces.

◆ **Purpose (aims).** A clear purpose is what distinguishes a report from a mere collection of data. In an academic report your purpose is to respond to an assignment task. Depending on the subject and approach, that task might be to test a hypothesis (an unproven idea), gather new information or confirm or challenge previous research. The purpose needs to be quite specific. The purpose 'to learn more about communication' is so vague that it has little meaning. In the sample report below, the stated purpose is 'to help the Chamber formulate a vision for the town's future to inform future planning decisions'.

In a major report, the purpose may be broken down into parts as a series of **aims and objectives**. If, for example, the **broad aim** of a report was to test observations about Councillors' performance during local Council meetings, then the **related sub-aims** or **specific objectives** might be to assess the meeting's effectiveness, identify needs for training, compare behaviours and so on.

◆ **Literature review.** The literature review surveys relevant research. This review demonstrates that you have completed the necessary readings and are familiar with relevant concepts and previous findings. Two common approaches are to give a chronological overview of relevant research or to group the available research into various schools of thought, comparing and contrasting their relative strengths and weaknesses.

◆ **Need for investigation.** Research for the sake of knowledge is an acceptable purpose in academia. In business and government circles, however, it is important to demonstrate the significance and importance of the research and the benefits that may flow from the research investment.

◆ **Closing statement.** A closing statement can reinforce the immediate value of the study, qualify the work's limitations (especially the scope of the research it addresses) or indicate some wider implications. The scope of a customer satisfaction survey, for example, might be restricted to satisfaction with service only or to certain States or regions, depending on the company's requirements.

Method

Reports based on **primary research** (first-hand) may include a section briefly describing the method that was used to carry out the research.

Findings (or results)

In the findings or results section, data is presented in an organised way to be readily accessible. With qualitative research, group and order your findings in different sections under headings which reflect your research aims. With quantitative research, tables are helpful for presenting large amounts of detail. Where a table does not relate directly to your discussion but is of supplementary value, it can be included in an **appendix**.

The aim is to present a **clear overall picture** of the results and the **patterns** they show. For qualitative research, a brief summary at the head of the section will achieve this. For quantitative research, you can also use figures such as **bar charts and pie charts** to illustrate trends and patterns. Other figures such as **diagrams**, **photographs and drawings** are also very useful for this purpose.

Discussion

Data does not become **meaningful information** until it is **interpreted**. In the discussion section, present a detailed analysis of the data and seek to explain your observations. Even if no particular research theme was specified for the report, you may have found that a **pattern emerged** when you interpreted the data. In the discussion (and conclusion) sections you have an opportunity to **address your research aims** and demonstrate your **mastery of the detail**.

Start your discussion with a paragraph **summarising the results** if you haven't already done this in the Findings section. Remember to keep the discussion focused on the assignment instructions and research aims.

Discussion can **focus on**:

◆ Summarising results in the data which relate to the research aims
◆ Assessing the significance of those results. Do they support existing theories and precepts or are they unexpected?
◆ Linking possibly related causes

- Attempting to explain or account for unexpected results, or non-results
- Assessing the scope and the limitations of your findings
- Discussing further implications
- Predicting likely outcomes or trends in the future
- Examining possible complicating variables (ie. changeable factors which may have influenced the outcomes).

> **TIP:** Even if you fail to achieve an expected research outcome, you can still explore reasons for this and produce a very worthwhile report.

Conclusion

In the conclusion, briefly **recap your findings** and refer back to the purpose and research aims of the report. The discussion in this section should **follow logically** from your findings. The reader should be able to draw conclusions similar to yours based on the data you have presented and analysed.

As with essays, the best reports often **gather momentum**, so that your reader is not left wondering 'So what?' How successfully have the research aims been answered? What remains to be explained? What is likely to have caused these results? What implications do they have for various issues or theories associated with the subject? **Relate the findings** to your readings, to lecture materials, real-life applications and so on. As with the essay, it is generally not appropriate to introduce new material at this point.

Recommendations

Recommendations sections are the **key focus of interest** in business and governmental applications. Some reports feature the recommendations at the very start.

References

Referencing is a means of **acknowledging your sources**. In the References section, list all sources you have referred to or quoted in the report. Alternatively, this may be referred to as the Bibliography. Sometimes the References section is followed by a separate Bibliography, listing other sources used while researching the report which aren't referred to in the report itself.

Your assignments must be referenced both in the text itself and at the end, in a detailed listing of the sources. Nowadays, parenthetical systems such as the **Harvard System** and the **American Psychological Association (APA)** system are commonly used. The Harvard System is used throughout this book. Styles of punctuation can vary somewhat. Just make sure that you punctuate consistently, following the recommendations in the source you use.

Parenthetical systems such as Harvard quote the source in brackets in the text of the essay or report, giving the author's name, year of publication and page number. For example:

'According to one source (Grevilleux 1996: 234) ... '

The full bibliographic information is then given in the References or Bibliography section at the end of the assignment. For an example of a References section see the sample essay (page 11) or sample report (page 41).

Some disciplines such as English and History still prefer the more traditional system, using **numbered notes**. This consists of inserting a number in the text, which corresponds to a numbered note at the foot of the page or at the end of the document or chapter. If you are using common word processing software, this can be done quite easily. Look for the Insert menu and select 'Footnote'. The window which pops up should offer you the option of putting the note at the foot of the page or at the end of the document (ie. footnote or endnote respectively).[1] Type in the bibliographical information and/or other academic comment.

It is important to reference every source you use, as you may be accused of **plagiarism** (passing off another's work as your own). This is a matter that is taken very seriously. Referencing allows your marker to **check your sources** for themselves where necessary. Many educational institutions offer a free Style Guide which sets out the approved ways of quoting, citing sources and setting out reference and bibliography listings. Your Faculty, School or Department should be able to advise what system is preferred. However, check with each teacher/lecturer as preferences do vary.

Computer programs such as Endnote are available to make referencing easier. You may be able to download a free copy of the software from your institution's website. You may also find referencing guides on-line at your institution's library homesite or departmental web pages.

Appendices

An appendix provides **supplementary information** which is related to the report but not essential to the discussion. The appendix appears after the References and/or Bibliography sections. It can consist of policy statements, tables, figures, transcripts of interviews, blank or completed survey forms and other supporting information. Each appendix should have a separate title page, with title, authorship and publication details where appropriate.

---

[1] This is what a footnote looks like. A good resource for further information on referencing, including the citation of electronic material, is the *Style Manual for Authors, Publishers and Printers* (6th edn), Australia, 2002, Chapter 12.

The scientific report

The scientific report has the following **features**:

- Abstract
- Introduction
- Aim
- Method
- Results
- Conclusion/Discussion
- References
- Bibliography
- Appendices

A scientific report, such as a lab report, is **more rigidly structured** than other reports. It starts by stating the theory or hypothesis which is to be tested or the research question. It then documents how the research was conducted and measured, tabulates and analyses the results and draws a conclusion.

The report should contain sufficient information to allow others to **test the logic** of the reasoning and methodology and, if necessary, **replicate the experiment** and check the results.

Aim

In this section, the purpose of the research is outlined clearly and specifically. Testing a hypothesis is a common aim in scientific research.

Method

This section gives **a clear explanation** of what research was undertaken, how and why it was carried out. Details might include:

- Step-by-step description of the procedure
- Size and extent of study
- Participants: nature, number, how selected, where found
- Materials used
- How results were documented
- How results were analysed
- Reference to previous research.

Results

It is usual for scientific reports to provide relevant graphs, tables and statistical analyses to aid the interpretation and discussion.

Conclusion/Discussion

If the research has been noteworthy, or even conclusive in some way, then this section may be headed 'Conclusion'. For less productive experiments the heading 'Discussion' may be used.

The business report

As with other report formats, at the heart of the business report lies its **purpose**. There are many different possible purposes. For example, **progress reports** are designed to assess how well a particular project is going, often halfway through that project. **Feasibility studies** assess whether a particular proposal is likely to succeed or not. **Incident reports** provide the details of some particular event for the purpose of informing interested parties and allowing them to assess the implications.

In a business report the closest attention is paid to the **'bottom line'**: what is the conclusion, and in particular, what are the recommendations. The **factual and analytical basis** for these recommendations should be found in the body of the report. Some businesses prefer to receive the **summary of recommendations** or **executive summary** at the start of the report. This is an extremely important part of the business report as it is designed to bring very busy decision-makers quickly 'up to speed'. It is usual for a substantial report to be sent with a covering letter or **'letter of transmittal'**. This is a letter from the author of a report or head of the reporting body to the person for whom the report is intended. It briefly **states the purpose** of the report. Depending on the parties involved, it may offer a personalised account of the findings and recommendations based on the needs of the busy reader.

The following is a very simple **example** of the business report format. While basic, it does illustrate aspects of this genre for the beginner.

Sample business report

SWOT Analysis: Cheston's business future in the face of a highway detour

For Cheston Chamber of Commerce and Industry

Executive summary

The Cheston Chamber of Commerce and Industry commissioned a SWOT analysis (Strengths Weaknesses Opportunities Threats) with a view to meeting the challenges faced by local businesses in light of the re-routing of the main highway away from the town. The analysis reveals that while this major change has the potential to affect the local economy severely, the town has great opportunities to build on other strengths. It is suggested that the Cheston Chamber of Commerce and Industry examine the feasibility of the town 'branding' itself as a small tourist destination: a charming town with heritage and history, located away from the bustling tourism mainstream.

Introduction

Cheston is a small coastal town directly on the route of a highway that serves some major tourist destinations. Cheston itself however is little known, and the town's businesses mostly attract only local trade and 'convenience' passing trade from outside the town. Cheston has been neglected for decades owing to long-standing plans to build the new section of highway, destined to detour the town by a couple of kilometres.

Background info

The Cheston Chamber of Commerce and Industry commissioned a consultant to undertake a SWOT analysis in consultation with the local community. The purpose was to help the Chamber formulate a vision for the town's future to inform future planning decisions. It was felt that a suitable response to the great challenge ahead would not simply 'fall into place' but must be planned.

Purpose

Need

Method

A focus group was convened to bring together as wide as possible a range of 'stakeholders' in the town: local landholders, shopkeepers, businesses in the industrial area, local activist groups, the Parents and Citizens committees of local schools, youth representatives and the elderly. The purpose was to explore a wide range of ideas with the ultimate aim of brokering a united vision that would be acceptable to the majority of local people.

Suggestions were written on butcher's paper and displayed on the wall for all to see. Participants were then asked to shortlist a maximum of six important factors in each category. A second workshop was held two weeks later, to establish some specific objectives.

Results

The shortlists under each category are as follows:

Strengths

◆ Community loyalty to local shops

- Low-key tourist attractions: beach, bushwalks, tourist shops, old pub, etc
- Community centre servicing wider local area: library, health centre, community centre, hall, parks
- Approaches to village from north and south are visually appealing
- Unique heritage: intact streetscape, interesting old buildings
- Rich history

Weaknesses

- Long neglect of buildings and streetscape lessens visual appeal of town
- Uncertainty over effects of new highway has paralysed future planning
- Poor recognition of Cheston compared to 'big name' towns
- Hard to get Council to commit resources to Cheston owing to uncertainty over future
- Local pessimism
- Lack of a creative vision for the future

Opportunities

- Rerouting of highway allows for a quieter ambience; more attractive for city dwellers to 'get away from it all'
- Chance to 'brand' Cheston as an untouched, unique destination
- Can restore heritage to return some of the town's original charm
- Small tourism opportunities: bed and breakfast, heritage and green tourism
- Build on community focus to stage local 'drawcard' events such as markets, concerts etc
- Guesthouses and a convention centre could attract city business people

Threats

- Loss of passing traffic to new highway, loss of passing trade
- Danger of becoming a 'ghost town' and losing local residents
- 'Do nothing' option would be seen as admission of defeat
- Some businesses may no longer be viable
- Local industrial area may suffer because no longer on major trucking routes

Discussion

With the new highway route imminent, most locals believed that it was important to plan for the future and that the 'do nothing' option would be disastrous. With the local Council about to undertake consultation for the development of a new environmental management plan, it was seen as essential to present the Council with a new vision for the town that enjoyed widespread community support.

Inevitably, there were widely differing views; a number of locals expressed extreme pessimism about the future of the town, and some business owners could see little prospect of their business surviving the change. The majority of stakeholders however felt that 'branding' Cheston as a unique and historic haven by the sea would be the most appropriate future for the town. There was strong sentiment that some kind of main street restoration program could work extremely well (see Vines, 1996).

Conclusion

The majority of participants, from a wide range of interest groups, felt that Cheston should take advantage of the highway bypass to promote itself as a small tourism destination, emphasising its uniqueness and charm, heritage and history and its potential as a refuge from more crowded, noisier destinations. While the idea had some critics, most participants agreed that this plan had the strongest arguments in its favour.

Recommendations

At a second workshop, the results of the SWOT analysis were reviewed and ideas for specific measures were brainstormed, then shortlisted. The following proposals were accepted as initial steps that the Cheston Chamber of Commerce and Industry should lobby for or implement:

1 Committing funds to lifting the town's profile: website, street postings, tourist information centre and so on
2 Creating promotional materials and advertising in tourist publications
3 Seeking investment in new, tourist-oriented businesses: touring, arts and crafts etc
4 Creating incentives for owners of heritage buildings to restore them sympathetically
5 Putting up signage for local sites of heritage interest
6 Seeking further support from the State tourism authority.

References

Vines, E. (1996). *Streetwise: A Practical Guide for the Revitalisation of Commercial Heritage Precincts.* Peacock Publications for the National Trust, Norwood, South Australia.

THE GRADE APPROACH TO REPORT WRITING

The **five steps** to writing a report are summed up in the GRADE approach:

1 **G**et started with a plan
2 **R**esearch the report
3 **A**rrange and analyse
4 **D**raft the report
5 **E**dit: revise and rewrite.

Let us follow the progress of a group of Professional Communication students as they plan and carry out a research project assignment using the GRADE approach.

1 Get started with a plan

The group started planning their report from the day they were given the following assignment:

> In a small group, undertake primary research into one of the following topics:
>
> ◆ Conflict resolution
> ◆ Interpersonal skills
> ◆ Meeting behaviour
>
> Write a business report based on your findings. Your research should be focused on testing a theory, a set of principles or observation that you have encountered during your studies in Professional Communication or for the purpose of assessing communication practice in a workplace or other formal context. There must also be a component of secondary research in your report.

| Instruction keyword |
| Choice of 3 topic keywords |
| More instruction words |
| Subject |

NOTE: Report assignment instructions can contain **key words**, similar to those found in essay questions. In the above assignment, the **instructions** are to undertake primary research, with the purpose of testing a theory, set of principles or an observation. The **topic** comprises a choice of three options, while the particular **aspect** is left unspecified. The broad **subject** is professional communication practice and the report should reflect this.

Reports emphasise **research and the interpretation** of data. The student group therefore needed to plan well in advance, to give them time to gather the data, present it, analyse it and then write their report.

Explore the research question

The first step for the **student group** was to work out what the specific research aims were. What did they plan to find out? Like an essay question, **assignment instructions** may be quite specific or quite general. If it has a **specific research focus**, it is important to ensure that the research, discussion and conclusion all reflect this.

The first idea that arises may not be the best response to the assignment task. The student group therefore brainstormed a wide range of ideas, making a **list of specific aspects** to explore as well as possible different approaches. (Individuals planning a report can brainstorm ideas with classmates or colleagues.)

Select the research topic

Having developed a shortlist of research topics, the student group had to decide which one to choose. They eventually decided that **'meeting behaviour'** was the topic which interested them the most.

> ▶ **TIP:** Choose whichever topic interests you the most, not what sounds the easiest. You will enjoy researching and writing it more and are likely to achieve a better mark. If you cannot make up your mind which topic to choose:
>
> ◆ Do a quick survey of resources available on each topic
> ◆ Draw up an outline plan for each topic to test for feasibility.

Define research aims

Never try to cover every aspect of the topic – just take one manageable aspect and cover it in sufficient detail. Since 'Meeting behaviour' was too broad an area, the student group had to **narrow it down**. The group agreed that what interested them most about meeting behaviours was the different roles people play in meetings including the 'chatterer', the 'destroyer' and the 'egotist'. Further discussion and research narrowed the focus further to one small section in the course reader which discussed the following **three different orientations** of meeting behaviours:

◆ **'Task oriented'** behaviours aim to get the objectives of the meeting completed without necessarily worrying too much about other people's feelings and wishes.
◆ **'Group oriented'** behaviours aim to support the group as a whole by maintaining harmony and encouraging interaction.

◆ **'Individual oriented'** behaviours are self-centred behaviours designed to meet the personal needs of a certain person, at the expense of the meeting's purpose and the group's needs. The team decides to explore this theory in some real-life meetings.

TIMELINE FOR PRIMARY RESEARCH REPORT DUE IN 4 WEEKS

Wk	Mon	Tues	Weds	Thurs	Fri	Sat	Sun
1	Day 1	Day 2	Day 3	Day 4	Day 5	Day 6	Day 7
	Assignment given out: explore question, narrow it down, set research aims	Find research materials: borrow books, photocopy articles etc. Quickly skim read	Design and plan primary research	Read research materials, take notes	Read research materials, take notes		
2	Day 8	Day 9	Day 10	Day 11	Day 12	Day 13	Day 14
	Pilot primary research, revise design	Undertake primary research	Arrange and order information	Present information: tables, graphs etc.	Analyse information		
3	Day 15	Day 16	Day 17	Day 18	Day 19	Day 20	Day 21
	Plan report	Draft report	Further reading/re-reading	Revise report, work on weak areas	Refine language, check data and referencing		
4	Day 22	Day 23	Day 24	Day 25	Day 26	Day 27	Day 28
	Final draft	Final research and re-reading	Check presentation and format of report	Final revision of report	Proofread hard copy, print good copy, attach cover sheet, title page, appendices		
5	Day 29						
	Submit essay on time						

2 Research the report

Plan the research

Good reports must be well researched and the more clearly defined your research aims and the better planned your research, the better it is likely to be. Before finalising their research aims, the student team had to examine relevant **secondary research**. This is the first stage of research which involves consulting **works already written** on the subject being researched. This can include books, academic journals, newspapers and magazines, encyclopaedias, course outline, course readers, etc. A summary of past research can form a literature review in the introductory sections of the report.

The assignment question also required the student group to undertake **primary research**. This involves original research such as:

◆ Observations from a field visit
◆ Laboratory tests and experiments
◆ Focus groups, interviews, surveys, questionnaires
◆ Other experiments.

The student group decided to observe some public, local Council meetings. Their **research plan** involved:

◆ Revising all course materials related to meetings
◆ Conducting secondary research on meeting behaviours using textbooks and other sources
◆ Narrowing research aims
◆ Reading Council brochures, local papers and archives
◆ Devising means of measuring and recording results
◆ Observing a local Council meeting and piloting the research
◆ Refining the research methods
◆ Conducting primary research
◆ Checking and analysing findings.

Design the research

If there is little or no information on a particular topic you may need to design the research yourself. Take great care in this because ill-considered research design and methods will **distort or invalidate** the research: 'rubbish in, rubbish out' as the saying goes. For instance, a survey of customer evaluations of a particular product is NOT an objective guide to its qualities, but only a **measure of customer perceptions** at a given time and place.

If your research aim is to evaluate the product itself, you need a very different research design to test its qualities and performance. A good introduction to qualitative and quantitative research design can be found in Anderson and Poole (1998: 24–29).

3 Arrange and analyse

You need to organise your data by grouping and ordering it in an appropriate way (see pages 24–26). The report also requires you to present your data effectively and analyse it.

Present information

A good report presents and explains information clearly so that the results, trends, issues and exceptions are **easily accessible**.

Reports may present motor vehicle accident statistics; trends in home lending, credit consumption and household debt; surveys of injuries in the workplace; or voting patterns. You should **summarise** the overall results, point out **notable patterns** and/or unexpected results. The student group presented information on patterns of group-oriented and individual-oriented behaviour amongst Councillors for purposes of comparison in terms of outcomes.

The student group also considered various **graphic options** for presenting their information. Having measured and tabulated behaviours they used tables and graphs to summarise the results of their observations. **Graphs**, for example, are good for showing trends over time at a glance, such as changes in the rate of hospital visits for a particular illness. Graphs can also be used to compare two or more related variables such as the number of new mortgages issued and interest rates.

Tables organise a mass of information in a manageable format. **Pie charts** are useful for showing proportions – for example, where the various slices of the funding pie are spent. **Percentages**, **ratios and statistical measures** are useful in some subjects.

Analyse information

A good report analyses the data not by merely demonstrating the broad pattern of results but by examining the **causes and implications** as well. To 'analyse' means to separate a thing into its component parts. When we analyse, we start to understand what causes certain effects or what 'makes something tick'. One **analytical tool** that is often helpful is to trace the origins and the history of what you are studying.

The student group discussed the reasons for the dominance of group oriented behaviour in Council meetings and the problems created by individual oriented behaviour. They also highlighted difficulties they experienced in interpreting the data.

An important aid to analysis is **critical thinking**, which means not taking any concept or result for granted but independently examining it by **identifying and questioning assumptions** and **testing conclusions** against the known facts. Our first hunch is not necessarily right. We cannot assume that because one event occurred after another, it was therefore caused by that previous event. If we believe there is a causal link, we need to **establish the evidence**.

The student group, for example, did not just assume that behaviours were based solely on individual Councillors' personalities – issues such as group dynamics, corporate culture and political issues were also considered as motivators. Their conclusions were **tested** against established models and theories of individual and group behaviours in meetings.

As another example, the boom in housing prices in Australia in 2002 can be causally linked, among other factors, to low interest rates and government financial incentives for first home buyers.

The **first step** in analysing information is to check **what your results actually demonstrate** as distinct from what **general impression** you may have received. For example, our research team observing Council meetings may have come away with the impression that the meetings had been disorderly and destructive. Analysis of the data might reveal the opposite case: that the meetings as a whole were quite effective and their impression was caused by the colourful behaviour of just two Councillors.

The **second step** is to **find patterns and to account for them**. For example, if a customer survey for a national company shows far less satisfaction with service in one State than in others, this suggests problems with the service in that State. If satisfaction with the product itself, an air conditioner, for example, is at a similar level in all but one State, we have to explore reasons for this difference. The student group found that the greater the incidence of individual oriented behaviour among Councillors, the fewer positive outcomes for ratepayers were achieved. This suggested that aspects of corporate culture and meeting dynamics within Council required remedial action.

A top academic report will use the analytical tools, concepts and terminology **appropriate to the subject**. For example, marketing students may devise a market research survey and report based on a recommended approach. Science students may employ mathematical tools.

It is important to relate your analysis back to the research purpose. What were you attempting to discover or achieve? Did you achieve this? Were the results expected? What can you conclude as a result?

4 Draft the report

Make an outline plan

Once you have finished arranging and analysing your data, draft the report. Complete an **outline plan** first to establish the structure and give the report a meaningful shape. Before drawing up a plan, refer back to the assignment instructions. The student group drew up the following plan:

- ◆ **Executive Summary**
- ◆ **Introduction:**
  - – Importance of meetings
  - – Difficulty in making them effective and democratic
  - – Need for optimal outcomes based on appropriate behaviour
- ◆ **Literature Search:**
  - – Meeting roles and behaviours
  - – Appropriate procedures and behaviour
  - – Focus: orientation of behaviours
- ◆ **Method:**
  - – How behaviours have been measured and tabulated
  - – Trialling the method
- ◆ **Findings:**
  - – Summary of results
  - – Tables
  - – Graphs
- ◆ **Discussion:**
  - – Reasons for dominance of group oriented behaviour
  - – The problem of individual oriented behaviour
  - – Problems in interpreting the data
- ◆ **Conclusion:** some problems in meeting behaviour, especially if habitual
- ◆ **Recommendations:** need for Councillor awareness and training
- ◆ **References:**
- ◆ **Appendices:**
  - – Appendix 1: Summary of measured behaviours, by group
  - – Appendix 2: Bennington Council Standing Orders 2001
  - – Appendix 3: Bennington Council Briefing paper 87/2001 The Role of Councillor

Draft in format

If you use a computer, you can **copy and paste** your plan for use as a template for the report. It is advisable to set up the **format** from the start: headers and/or footers, line spacing, margins and so on. As a suggestion, use 1.5 line spacing and generous margins (preferably 3–4 centimetres) to allow space for the marker's comments. Check with your teacher, lecturer or learning institution to find out about **presentation requirements**. At work, enquire about house styles.

Label and number all graphs and figures and refer to them in the text. For tables, supply a heading, such as 'Table 2: Interest rates compared to housing prices in Australia 1980-2000'. Captions for figures (any graphic content other than tables) are generally placed below the figure. Photographs and computer-scanned images are also commonly used.

Use **headings** to break up your information into **manageable chunks**. If a particular section has a number of strands, arrange them logically under the main heading. In long reports it is common to mark heading levels with a **numbering system.** You can use either the decimal system or a number and letter system.

The hierarchy of headings can be signalled by other **visual strategies.** For example, major section headings may be capitalised, subsection headings in title case (key words beginning with a capital letter), and sub subheadings in lower case (non-capital) letters with only the first letter capitalised. Enhancements include bold type, centering and larger fonts.

Here are some suggestions for **drafting the different sections** of your report.

- **Abstract, Executive Summary or Summary**. Try drafting this section early to help **clarify your purpose**. Make sure that it echoes the instructions you have been given. Revise it once the final report is finished.
- **Introduction**. The introduction effectively starts the report. It provides the **necessary background** so that a reader who is not familiar with the topic will be able to understand what it is about. Do NOT simply repeat the abstract/summary.
- **Findings**. Be sure to **identify the patterns** which are evident – not merely present the data.
- **Discussion**. Relate your findings back to the assignment instructions and to your **research aims.** Have the findings achieved these aims? If not, why not? If so, to what extent? Qualify your findings by **considering variables** which might have affected the results. The student group, for example, considered the extent to which gender and cultural issues may have influenced their findings. Refer to theories or descriptive models which might explain your results. This is an opportunity to demonstrate that you understand the key concepts in the area you are discussing and are familiar with the relevant literature.
- **Conclusion**. Briefly **restate the overall findings**, referring to your research aims. Assess what you have managed to establish and what remains to be learnt. Depending on your instructions and the purpose of your report, it may be appropriate to add some **final comments**. As with the essay, it is advantageous to give your report a strong finish. For example:
  - Where the findings indicate further research is required, identify future research needs.

- Where the research has potential real-life implications, spell these out. If appropriate, **make recommendations**. The student group, for example, recommended promoting Councillor awareness of the effects of their behaviours and introducing appropriate training.

Check that your conclusion **relates to the assignment instructions** you were given. For example, the student group checked that their study of meeting behaviours answered the instructions regarding 'testing a theory, set of principles or observation ... for the purpose of assessing communication practice in a workplace or other formal context' (see page 45).

5 Edit: revise and rewrite

Leave yourself a day or two to refresh your mind, then read over the draft report. Start with the 'macro' issues relating to structure and content and only then look at the finer points of language such as grammar, spelling, punctuation and so on (see the language checklist on pages 59–60). The following **report checklist** offers a guide to revision. Not all items will necessarily apply to your report.

Report checklist

General
✓ Are teacher/lecturer specifications met?
✓ Are data and discussion relevant to purpose?
✓ Is the tone appropriate (factual and objective)?
✓ Have you used full sentences, not note form?
✓ Would it be understandable to a reader unfamiliar with the subject?
✓ Are judgements and assertions supported by evidence?
✓ Are the correct format and specified headings used, and is it set out like a report?

Abstract/Executive Summary
✓ Does it summarise the entire report?
✓ Is it brief: preferably one paragraph, no more than three?

Introduction
✓ Does it provide a broad overview/background before addressing its current purpose?
✓ Does it state a specific purpose and objectives (if not stated in a separate Aims section)?
✓ Does it have a literature review (and theoretical background)?
✓ What is the need for the investigation?
✓ Is there a closing statement (where applicable)?

Method (Scientific format)
- ✓ Is it logical and specific?
- ✓ Could a reader test your method and attempt a similar experiment?
- ✓ Is the method used appropriate to meet the research aims?

Findings/Results
- ✓ Are relevant results summarised?
- ✓ Is the heading hierarchy system and/or numbering system consistent?
- ✓ Are tables, graphs and figures numbered, labelled and referred to in text?

Discussion
- ✓ Is data presented clearly and information organised logically?
- ✓ Is data interpreted and analysed?
- ✓ Are findings related to purpose and research aims?
- ✓ Are the reliability and limitations of data assessed?
- ✓ Are possible complicating variables considered?

Conclusion
- ✓ Does it restate the overall picture of results?
- ✓ Are assignment instructions and research aims answered?
- ✓ Are judgements balanced and based on objective evidence?
- ✓ Do closing statements look at real life applications, suggest further research or add other final comments?
- ✓ Are recommendations called for?

References/Bibliography
- ✓ Is the specified referencing system used both in the text and in References/Bibliography?

Final checks
- ✓ Have you checked pagination, spelling, grammar and punctuation?
- ✓ Is there a cover sheet, title page and contents page (long reports)?
- ✓ Are appendices preceded by a title page and headings?

FURTHER TIPS FOR SUCCESS

Exam essays

Since you don't have time to draft and redraft **essays in an exam**, preparation and planning are of paramount importance. Here are some **strategies** you can employ:

- Make sure you **read all instructions** and follow them **exactly**. (It's easy to overlook something important.)
- Read the whole paper over quickly. Where there's a choice, start to think about **which questions** you'll answer and how to answer them.
- Sketch a quick **essay plan** for each question you will attempt before starting to write the essay. Sometimes forgotten information will 'click into place' when you come back to the question or you may find the inspiration which evaded you at first. Do not spend a long time on this – no more than a couple of minutes per question.
- If you get stuck on one essay, **quickly go on** to the others before coming back to it.
- If it's an open book exam, study your books thoroughly beforehand and **mark key information** with highlighters and post-it stickers so you can find the information quickly.
- Know in advance **how much time** is allowed for each question and **stick to it**. It may be tempting to write extra on one question which you know a lot about. However, the gains will be minimal compared to the marks you might lose if the answer to the next question is incomplete.
- Look at how many marks each question is worth and **tailor the length of your response** and the amount of time you spend on it accordingly. If a four-part question is worth twelve marks and Part A is worth three marks, you should spend about a quarter of the total time allocated to that question on that Part.
- Make doubly sure that you are not only **answering the question** but that you are answering ALL of it. If the question makes two or more demands, address all of them.
- Try to finish each essay **under time**, so you can check it over, fixing up any glaring omissions or errors.

Language issues

Getting help with writing

Writing language is much harder than speaking it. If you receive feedback that your language needs work, you should consider seeking additional help. Most universities and TAFES have specialised **learning assistance centres** where well-trained staff offer services for free, while schools may have an **academic support person**. Learning centres are open to anyone who wants to achieve more of their potential. They are well prepared to help students with non-English speaking backgrounds and people with specialised needs. They tend to get very busy, so you should book well ahead where possible.

Frequently asked questions

Can I use 'I'? Avoid using 'I' unless the assignment clearly requires you to advance a personal opinion or to refer to your own experience. The first person (as it is called) is neither ungrammatical nor 'wrong', but some teachers dislike its use in academic writing.

Some alternatives:

> It is the belief of this writer that … (I believe that …)
> It is likely that … (I think it is likely that …)
> It can be argued that … (I think it can be argued that …)
> The significance of the issue cannot be taken lightly … (I do not think we can take it lightly that …)
> In the experience of many professionals … (Professionals agree with me that …)

Can I start a sentence with 'and' or 'but'? Generally, avoid this. The purpose of conjunctions like these is to join two clauses in the one sentence. However, many people ignore this rule nowadays.

Can I use contractions? Contractions are short forms of a word or words. In academic writing it is best to write words in full. Instead of 'isn't' write 'is not'. 'Can't' becomes 'cannot', 'shouldn't' becomes 'should not' and so on.

Why is the passive voice a problem? There are two main ways of 'voicing' a sentence. The so-called **active voice** places the subject of the sentence as the active agent whereas the **passive voice** places the subject as the person or thing which 'undergoes the process or actions expressed in the verb' (Peters, 1995: 567). For example:

- ◆ **Active voice:** In future, you (subject) will empty (verb) all rubbish bins on Friday.
- ◆ **Passive voice:** In future, rubbish bins are to be emptied by you on Friday. (The passive voice emphasises the action rather than the doer.)

◆ **Passive voice:** In future, bins are to be emptied on Friday. (This version avoids the question 'Who is going to do it?')

Both the active voice and the passive voice are perfectly grammatical and the passive voice has a valuable role in scientific writing, business writing, academia and elsewhere. However, **overuse of the passive voice** can make formal language **dense and obscure.** Generally, the active voice is **preferred for clarity** and that is why grammar checkers query the passive.

The following is an example of **misuse of the passive:**

> *An investigation into the misuse of funds was decided to be carried out by the manager.*

The above sentence is awkward in the extreme. It would have been better to use the active voice:

> *The manager decided to investigate the misuse of funds.*

What is a split infinitive? A so-called split infinitive is where words are inserted between 'to' and the verb in the infinitive form. For example:

> *I need to quickly assess the issues.*

Some teachers consider this a problem and for that reason it is suggested you avoid it. However, authorities such as Pam Peters (1995: 711) recommend using the split infinitive where the result is less cumbersome than not splitting it.

Grammar

Many people use **grammar checks** on their computers. Treat them as helpful prompts to guide you but **not as infallible experts** to be relied upon. Only you (or a helpful mentor) can decide if the language use is appropriate in context. If you are unsure, refer to a good English grammar text. (See Further Reading, page 61.)

Punctuation

Poor punctuation can completely change your meaning.

Apostrophes. A common error is the misuse of apostrophes. Apostrophes are NOT used to indicate the plural. Apostrophes are used in:

1 The possessive case – Jane's car, mum's telephone.
2 Contractions (two words shortened into one) – it's, don't, isn't, can't, won't and so on.

Where you place the apostrophe is important. When a noun is singular in the possessive case, an apostrophe is inserted before the last letter. For example: 'The engine belonging to the car is the **car's** engine'. However, when a noun is **plural in the possessive case**, the apostrophe is inserted after the last letter. For example: 'The engines belonging to several vehicles are the **cars'** engines'. The regular plural of car is 'cars' – no apostrophe!

Colons. Colons are used to introduce items: a list of things or facts, a quotation or some other matter, as in:

> *Always remember the three 'Ps' of real estate: Position, Position and Position.*

> *Winston said: 'Believe in me'.*

Commas. Commas are much abused. Their main purpose is to separate items in a list or to mark off one thought from another. They are not a type of full stop nor do they have to be inserted every few words just to give the reader a chance to breathe!

The comma is **rightly placed** here:

> *The purpose of this statement is to comfort readers, empowering them with a sense of ability.*

The comma is **wrongly placed** here:

> *Readers, who are disturbed, will be moved to react violently by this advertisement.*

The first comma implies that all readers are disturbed.

Don't use commas in place of a full stop:

> *The language conveys to the readers a sense of respect, despite the appalling living conditions she is proud of her achievements.*

A full stop should replace the comma in the above example.

Run-on sentences. Run-on sentences push on well beyond the logical point where one sentence ends and the next begins without a full stop words soon start to pile up meaninglessly in a disorganised jumble.

The above sentence should stop at the word 'begins'!

Semi-colons. Semi-colons are 'half a full stop because (they) can always be replaced by one' (Whitaker-Wilson, 1958: 19). Sometimes it is better to use a semi-colon than a full stop; it can join two related thoughts together in one sentence and establish a link, as it does in this sentence.

Spelling. Accurate spelling looks professional, whereas misspellings can cause you embarrassment! One word consistently misspelt looks like multiple errors. Good spelling comes from active memory work. Some suggestions for good spelling are:

◆ Make lists of words you have misspelt, and ask someone to test you occasionally. Once you get them right on **three separate occasions** in a row, cross them off your list.

◆ One memory device for **tricky spellings** is to say the word aloud phonetically (as it looks when written down) rather than how it is meant to sound. How would you pronounce the word 'sword' for instance? How would you pronounce 'answer'?

◆ **Spell checkers** are a helpful prompt but will let through many errors. On many occasions I have found my American software's 'corrections' to be quite wrong for Australia. Often the 'correction' suggested is the wrong word altogether. Unwary use of spell checkers can produce some **bizarre results**. They cannot tell you when to spell 'affect' rather than effect, 'insure' rather than ensure, or advise whether to use 'to', 'two' or 'too'. And the list goes on ...

Non-discriminatory language

Language often carries various **connotations** (secondary meanings), and one can cause offence unknowingly by being thoughtless. So-called **'PC' language** is not merely politically correct but also Polite and Courteous. **Sexist language** is one of the most common traps; older literature is loaded with references to 'mankind', to 'the works of Man' and so on. The term **'settlement of Australia'** in reference to the European era, for example, is an offensive term to many Indigenous persons. University style guides generally offer advice on appropriate terminology. When you write, remember that persons of different gender, race, religion or age may see things very differently to yourself.

Language checklist

✓ Have you used **complete sentences** rather than note form?
✓ Are any **words** left out?
✓ Have you spelt out **acronyms** the first time you've used them, eg. 'National Roads and Motorists Authority (NRMA)'?
✓ Is the expression **clear and simple**, not padded with unecessary words?

- ✓ Is the tone **formal and objective**, rather than personal?
- ✓ Have you removed any colloquial language or **slang**?
- ✓ Have you used **appropriate language** for the subject?
- ✓ Do you know the **meaning** of all the words in your work?
- ✓ Have you used **punctuation** (commas, semi-colons, colon, quotation marks) correctly?
- ✓ Has the spelling of **difficult words** been checked in a dictionary?
- ✓ Have you checked for **grammatical mistakes** you are in the habit of making?
- ✓ Is the language **non-discriminatory** in terms of race, religion, age and gender?

Final words

The GRADE approach suggested in this book is a **starting point only**. There are many rules on the essay and report forms and language use, but few relating to the **process of writing**.

A good approach to writing is one that inspires your imagination, stimulates the learning process and delivers the slow satisfaction of a job well done. The more you write and the more you read, the better writer you will become.

FURTHER READING AND RESOURCES

Academic writing

Anderson, J. and Poole, M. (1998). *Assignment and Thesis Writing* (3rd edn). John Wiley and Sons, Brisbane.

Bate, D. and Sharpe, P. (1996). *Writer's Handbook for University Students* (2nd edn). Nelson Thomson Learning, Melbourne.

Lovel, D. (2001). *Macquarie Student Writer's Friend: A Guide to Essay Writing*. The Macquarie Library, Sydney.

McLaren, S. (1997). *Quicksmart EasyWriter: A Student's Guide to Writing Essays and Reports*. Pascal Press, Sydney.

Language

Burton, S.H. (1984). *Mastering English Grammar*. Macmillan, London.

Eagleson, R.D. (1990). *Writing in Plain English*. AGPS, Canberra.

Murray-Smith, S. (1987). *Right words: A Guide to English Usage*. Viking, Melbourne.

Peters, P. (1995). *The Cambridge Australian English Style Guide*. Cambridge University Press, Victoria.

Strunk, W. and White, E.B. (1979). *The Elements of Style* (3rd edition). Macmillan, New York.

Swan, M. (1980). *Practical English Usage*. Oxford University Press, Oxford.

Thomson, A.J. and Martinet, A.V. (1986). *A Practical English Grammar*. Oxford University Press, Oxford.

Whitaker-Wilson, C. (1975). *Punctuation*. Sun Books, South Melbourne.

Williams, J.M. (1994). *Style: Ten Lessons in Clarity and Grace*. Harper Collins, New York.

Other resources

Dictionaries: *Macquarie Dictionary* is a key Australian reference. *Chambers Twentieth Century Dictionary* is also recommended.

Thesauruses: B. Kirkpatrick (ed.) (1987), *The Authorised Roget's Thesaurus*, Penguin, London.

Style guides: Australian Government Publishing Service (2002). *Style Manual for Authors, Editors and Printers of Australia* (6th edn). John Wiley and Sons, Australia.

Websites: You will find numerous helpful websites, including Strunk and White's *The Elements of Style, Bartlett's Quotations*, on-line dictionaries, grammar sites and so on, on the world wide web. Search for them using search engines such as Google, Lycos, Yahoo and so on. ANZWERS is one good Australian search engine: http://www.anzwers.com.au. The University of Western Sydney Library website has various helpful links such as the Australian Libraries Gateway and World Libraries: http://library.uws.edu.au/catalogues_index.phtml and http://library.uws.edu.au/online/citing.phtml

GLOSSARY

Argument: Usually the basis of an essay, it develops a proposition, supporting it with evidence and detailed discussion and bringing it to a conclusion.

Bibliography: A list of works placed at the end of an essay or report, giving author, title and publication details. Often referred to as 'References'.

Brainstorm: A strategy to create many ideas in response to a problem; best done in groups.

Criterion: (plural, **criteria**): Means of measurement, choice or evaluation.

Exposition: One of the four modes of writing: 'explaining'. The other modes are description, narration and argument.

Genre: A form of writing. Essays and reports are examples of genres. Each genre has its own features and rules.

Hierarchy of headings: The order of headings, signalled by visual cues in a report.

Hypothesis: A working theory, a proposition not yet given.

Literature review: A survey of relevant research.

Plagiarism: Representing another person's work as your own.

Primary research: Research to collect or generate new data.

Proposition: The central idea your essay seeks to argue.

Qualify: To limit one's conclusions according to available facts and logical assessment.

Qualitative research: Research based on subjective assessments.

Quantitative research: Research based on countable, objective data.

References: System of acknowledging sources both within text and in a detailed list at the end of the essay or report.

Research aims: In reports, the focus of your research, the specific question you attempt to answer.

Secondary research: Review of existing published information.

Scope: The range or limit of your assignment.

Topic sentence: A sentence that states the main theme of a paragraph.

Thesis: Similar to 'proposition'. In this guide it refers to a proposition supplied by a student rather than one suggested by the essay question. (Not to be confused with the written volume created by Honours or postgraduate research students.)

Variable: Changeable factor. When analysing results, consider what variables may have influenced outcomes. For example, when looking at attendance figures for major sporting events, it is possible that weather conditions had some bearing on low attendance.

INDEX